HEY DOG! LET'S TALK!

'This book is a little masterpiece of concise advice to help all children understand and make friends with the right dogs. Most importantly, it advises simply and clearly how children (and adults too) can recognise dogs that are unsure in unfamiliar human company or that aren't willing to be approached and handled, and so stay safe around them. The straightforward text and delightful illustrations enable children to learn how dogs communicate their feelings and intentions and so understand how they should respond to canine facial and body language signals. This helps them appreciate all the benefits of having dogs as friends and family, and will also help many dogs feel more comfortable around children because they will have been approached in a calm and respectful manner. A must-have little book for all parents and would-be parents if you are intending to bring a new puppy or dog into your family, or simply want to help your kids be safe with dogs in society and enjoy their occasional company'.

Professor Peter Neville, Director,
Centre of Applied Pet Ethology (COAPE), UK, Poland and South Africa

This book needs to be on the National Curriculum and taught in every primary school in the country. The UK dog population stands at around 8.5 million, 1 in 4 families have a dog and most of these dogs are much loved members of the family. The benefits for children of loving and caring for a pet dog are well-established and far-reaching. For example, there is a linkage between being kind to dogs when young and being kind and caring towards people too in adulthood. Yet, only 16% of children are taught anything about basic animal welfare at school. However, dog-ownership is not without risk. In the UK around 1.5 million people are bitten by a dog every year and in half of these bites the victim is a child. Furthermore, most of these bites occur in the family home and the dog is the family pet, or a visiting dog known to the family. The science also tells us that the vast majority of these dog bites are the result of a mis-communication between the dog and the child and are thus easily preventable.

This is where 'Hey Dog' comes in. 'Hey Dog' cleverly achieves the rare combination of clear and concise messaging presented around interesting, light-hearted and funny stories. Kids will love reading this book and their adults will too!

Dr Robert Falconer-Taylor BVetMed, DipCABT, MRCVS
Veterinary Director and Head of Education

HEY DOG! LET'S TALK!

Wendy Keefer

Illustrations by Sarah Hobbs

The Book Guild Ltd

First published in Great Britain in 2018 by
The Book Guild Ltd
9 Priory Business Park
Wistow Road, Kibworth
Leicestershire, LE8 0RX
Freephone: 0800 999 2982
www.bookguild.co.uk
Email: info@bookguild.co.uk
Twitter: @bookguild

Copyright © 2018 Wendy Keefer
Illustrations © 2018 Sarah Hobbs

The right of Wendy Keefer to be identified as the author of this
work has been asserted by her in accordance with the
Copyright, Design and Patents Act 1988.

All rights reserved. No part of this publication may be
reproduced, transmitted, or stored in a retrieval system, in any form or by any means,
without permission in writing from the publisher, nor be otherwise circulated in
any form of binding or cover other than that in which it is published and without
a similar condition being imposed on the subsequent purchaser.

This work is entirely fictitious and bears no resemblance to any persons living or dead.

Typeset in Minion Pro

Printed and bound in Great Britain by CPI Group (UK) Ltd, Croydon, CR0 4YY

ISBN 978 1912575 534

British Library Cataloguing in Publication Data.
A catalogue record for this book is available from the British Library.

*From a little understanding,
heaps of love will grow.*

CONTENTS

PART ONE   I AM LISTENING!   1

PART TWO   I CAN TALK TO YOU!   11

PART THREE   IT'S YOUR CHOICE   21

PART ONE
I AM LISTENING!

Do you ever wonder what your dog would say if he could speak to you?

We speak with our voices, and gesture with our hands. We also use body language and facial expressions.

Dogs make sounds but mostly they talk to each other using their bodies and faces. The way they stand and the way they hold their heads and tails tell the other dog how they are feeling. They speak to us this way as well.

Sadly for dogs and the people who love them, misunderstandings can happen. A dog may think he is telling us clearly that he is unhappy but we don't see it. If he is frightened or angry he may have to use more direct action. Often this is a growl, sometimes it is a bite.

Here, Hey Dog is showing us what it looks like to be very frightened. You will see that his ears are back and his tail is low and he is showing his teeth. He is saying, "Don't come any closer, I don't want to have to bite you."

This time, Hey Dog is showing us what it looks like to be angry. His ears and tail are held high and he is showing his teeth again. On his back you will see his fur is standing up. This is called 'raised hackles'. He is saying, "Keep away!"

Dogs don't like being frightened or angry. If we learn to understand them we can all live safely and happily together. Hey Dog thinks this book is a great place to start!

WHAT DOES A WORRIED DOG LOOK LIKE?

A worried or nervous dog may turn his head away and avoid eye-contact. He is saying, "I won't hurt you if you don't hurt me!"

You might notice your dog is licking his lips even when he is not hungry. Hey Dog says, "I don't understand."

Yawning doesn't always mean, "I'm tired." To a dog it may mean, "I'm not very comfortable with this."

Look closely, can you see the whites of his eyes? If you can, it may mean he is not too sure he likes what's happening.

Poor Hey Dog is really scared! Have you noticed his tail is tucked between his legs? Even his head and ears are down!

The best thing you can do is back away slowly and give him space.

Not every dog shows worry in the same way. It can help to be aware of these little signs. If you see these signs, move back. If the dog is really saying, "I like what you are doing," he will come with you!

There is no mistaking this expression, however. This time Hey Dog is saying,

"I´M A HAPPY DOG!"

PART TWO
I CAN TALK TO YOU!

Understanding dogs can be difficult.
    There are big ones and small ones, hairy ones and smooth ones, friendly ones and shy ones. It is hard to believe they are all dogs sometimes!

We need to know how to stay safe even when we do not understand what the dog is saying.

Let us look at two dogs meeting each other for the first time.
  Here you will see that Hey Dog has stopped. He has turned sideways and is looking away from Goldie.

"Hey Dog, will you be my friend?"

Hey Dog is saying, "You can trust me."

We can talk to a dog in the same way. We also want to tell the dog he can trust us. We remember it by learning:

STAND STILL / HANDS DOWN
LOOK AWAY / WAIT

"Jonny, you need to wash your knees."

Jonny and his dog, Barker, show you how it looks.

WHAT DOES THIS MEAN TO THE DOG?

STAND STILL

I will not come any closer

HANDS DOWN

I will not hurt you

LOOK AWAY

I do not want a fight

WAIT

I will wait to see if you want to be friends or I will wait for a grown-up to come. If you wait long enough, the dog will go away.

Standing still works well with a new dog. It is also a good way to ask your own dog to calm down.
Some dogs may jump up or get too excited when you are playing with them.

"Come on, Lucy, let's play! Let's play!"

Lucy's dog, Snowy, gets very excited sometimes.

When that happens, she tries:

>STAND STILL / HANDS DOWN
>LOOK AWAY / WAIT

Her body says, "It is time to calm down," in a way her dog will understand.

"Oh, I get it. You want me to sit first."

What do you do if a dog knocks you down?
   Curl up in a ball!
   Danny has been knocked down by Ranger. He shows us how he:

STAYS STILL / DOESN'T LOOK / WAITS

"Sorry about that, Danny."

Like Ranger, your dog will soon know you do not want to play that game!
   You see? It is easy to talk like a dog!

PART THREE
IT'S YOUR CHOICE

Now you understand what your dog is saying and you know how to talk to him.

But there is another way for kids to stay safe around dogs. This is:

GIVING THE DOG A CHOICE

WHY IS THIS IMPORTANT?

"Gee, I hope there aren't any scary kids out there…"

The dog may be <u>afraid</u>.
    As we have learned, a frightened dog can bite.

The dog may be in <u>pain</u>.

"What? You want to play now? No thanks, maybe later."

The dog may be hurt or sick. Often, as a dog grows older, he can get painful joints or just be too tired to play.

The other reason we offer dogs choice is to help build trust.

"Mark is my very best friend!"

By showing the dog you respect his choice, you become a kid a dog can trust. So, how do you give a dog choice? It's simple. Ask him!

Instead of going to your dog, call him to you.
 Nancy will practice with Hey Dog. She stands a little way away, pats her leg and says,
 "Hey Dog! Do you want to come?"

"Did you say something about treats?"

If Hey Dog wants to come, he will.
 If he doesn't she will say, "That's ok, maybe next time."
 Do this and your dog will know he can trust you.

When would you give a dog this choice?
    A good time is when you meet a new dog.
    First, stand away and ask the owner permission to stroke her dog. If the answer is 'yes', pat your leg and say, "Hey dog, would you like to come see me?"

"He looks like a nice boy."

Remember, it's ok if she doesn't want to come.

If she chooses to come, it's important to only use one hand to stroke her. This way she won't feel she is being grabbed or held when she doesn't want to be. Think:

ONE HAND TOUCH
TWO HANDS TOO MUCH

"Ooh, lovely! That's my favourite spot!"

Try stroking her on her shoulder or scratching her chest. She'll like that.

With your own dog, there are lots of times you would give him the choice. Josie waits when Snoopy is on his bed.

"I feel nice and safe in my bed."

Spot is comfy on a chair so Nick stands away with his ball to see if he wants to play.

"Oh boy! It's Nick with my ball!"

Lizzie reads patiently while Ramble is eating. He will come to her when he is finished.

"Hang on a minute, Lizzie, I'm almost done!"

All of these dogs know they can trust their kids because they let the dog choose to come or stay where they are.
    Your dog will trust you too!